"Hurry up, Tony," called Diana through the open door. "I'm ready and Mitch is outside in the car." Her brother hurried across the room and picked up two large rucksacks.

"They feel too light," he said. "Have you packed everything—all the ropes, equipment and gear?"
"Of course I have, silly," said Diana. "Especially food and lots of hot drinks."

"Do be careful," said their older sister. "F c a

1

Outside they loaded the ropes, rucksacks and special equipment into the back of the car. It was a hot day, but they were all wearing heavy clothing, for it would be cold underground.

"Good-bye, Sis," called Tony. "Don't worry. We'll all be back in time for tea." Mitch had found a new cave he wanted to explore.
"We will look at the rocks," he said.

"I want to get some specimens and find out what minerals or metals are there." Mitch was a geologist and he was always studying rocks.

Later that morning they left the car, climbed down to the beach and put on their pot-holing gear.
'That's the place," said Mitch, as he pointed to a dark hole in the cliff.

As they entered the cave they put on their safety helmets, and then checked the ropes and rucksacks. Almost at once they were in complete darkness.

"My light's not working properly," said Diana. "Never mind, keep close to me," replied Tony in a whisper, for he knew Mitch would not have gone on with a faulty light.

3

Gradually the cave got narrower until they were forced to crawl along a tiny ledge of rock.
"Go carefully, and stay together," warned Mitch.
"One slip and . . ."

Diana and Tony knew only too well what he meant. Suddenly Tony called, "Look, there's water—it must be an underground river."

"Stay where you are," warned Mitch.
"Where you are. Where you are. Where you are." The echoes were stopped by a terrific splash as Tony hit the water.

Holding back a scream of terror that rose in her throat, Diana helped Mitch drag Tony out of the water. He was gasping for breath and shuddering with cold.

"Shall we go back?" asked Diana hopefully.
"No, I'm all right," said Tony.
"Now, perhaps you'll put a rope on, as I told you," warned Mitch.

They roped-up, and made their way carefully along the river bed. Suddenly, round a bend, they found themselves near another cave.

They climbed up out of the water and looked around. "There's someone there," screamed Diana, thinking of cavemen and monsters. "Don't be silly, it's only the shadow of a rock."

Mitch looked round the cave and found a small hole in the floor. He secured the rope to a small boulder and then said, "Tony and I will go down and explore. You can follow later."

Left alone with her thoughts, Diana made up her mind that she would never go pot-holing again.

Tony followed Mitch in the semi-darkness.

"We must be in a tunnel," said Mitch thoughtfully. "Man-made too. The cuts on the sides are too regular for a natural crack or fissure."

"Perhaps it's a mine," said Tony.

"An old mine for sure," replied Mitch. "We must be careful, old mines are very dangerous. Look at this."

He swung his torch up towards a rock which glittered in the light.

"I must get a piece," said Tony as he unroped.

"Can you see the colour?" he called as he climbed higher. "I must get several pieces." "Don't go higher," cried Mitch. "Stay where you are!"

But already Tony was at work with his hammer, removing small pieces. Then he saw an extra fine piece and leaned over to hammer it free.

"Look out!" warned Mitch.

Too late. Tony's boots slipped on the slimy rocks, and he came tumbling down, bringing much of the roof with him. His tangled body lay still on the floor.

"Tony! Tony! Are you all right?" asked Mitch as he gently groped about in the dust and darkness. Their light had gone out, and only the dim light from the helmet lamps remained.

Tony lay unconscious. Mitch searched for the way out but the hole was blocked. He pulled at the rocks but they were too heavy to move.

In a flash he realised their position. They would be lucky to get out alive. "Diana!" called Mitch. "We are trapped. We can't get out. Tony is hurt!"

Mitch clawed desperately at the rocks but they refused to move. Diana tried to help from the other side, but after a few minutes they were forced to give up.

"The rocks are too heavy to move," said Mitch. "We must have help. You must go for help, Diana!"

"But what about Tony?"

"I'll look after him," replied Mitch. "But you must go quickly." Diana thought of the darkness, and the murky underground river, and shivered.

"I don't know the way, but I'll try," she said. "Have you got your rucksacks with food and drink? I may be some time!"

"Yes, they are here," came the muffled reply.

Diana plunged into the darkness and tried to remember the way back. At last she reached the underground river.

Her light began to fade as she hurried along through the swirling water.

Later, shivering with cold, she saw a faint light through the darkness, and realised she was nearly at the mouth of the cave. Once outside, she ran along the beach for help.

She rushed up to the car but found it was locked. Mitch had got the key.

In despair she ran across the fields to a small cottage and pressed the bell again and again. Would they never answer?

Down in the tunnel Mitch waited patiently for help. Suddenly, Tony moved and opened his eyes. He felt sick and his left arm hurt. "It may be broken," said Mitch. "Let me feel it."

He tied up the arm with a handkerchief, and then told Tony that Diana had gone for help and that they must wait until she returned.

"But! But! Suppose she gets lost or falls in the river or . . ."
"Don't worry, son!" said Mitch. "She'll make it. You'll soon be back home safe and sound."

At last the farmer's wife opened the door.
"What is it, my dear?"
"Help! Quick! My brother, Mitch—they'll die!" Diana gasped out with big tears filling her eyes.

"Now, now, dear, take it easy and tell me what has happened; then I can help you." She picked up the telephone, and began to dial.

Diana drank a cup of hot tea, and wondered how Tony and Mitch were getting on down in the mine.

14

Diana heard the farmer's wife give all the information to the Special Rescue Service in a clear steady voice, and she felt much happier. About half an hour later two cars pulled up outside.

Four men loaded with special rescue equipment came to the door. The leader, Big Jim Taylor, asked Diana more questions about the cave.

"Must be Wrecker's Cave," he said. "Come with me." "Oh, please, please hurry!" said Diana. "Don't worry," smiled Big Jim. "We've never lost anybody yet!"

In the gloom of the tunnel, Mitch checked the food. "We must ration it out," he said. "We may have a long wait."

"How long?" asked Tony. "Can't say for sure," replied Mitch, "but they'll be here, don't you worry." Tony sat up. His arm ached badly, and he felt sick with the pain.

"Look," he said, "there's water on the floor. It's trickling down the walls. If they don't come soon the cave will fill up and we'll be drowned."

"Listen!" said Mitch as he jumped to his feet. "Listen! I can hear something. There! There! There it is again! It's a voice. It's Diana!"

"Tony, Mitch are you all right?" came the muffled sound through the rock. "Yes. Yes. We're here," they shouted back. Jim Taylor looked at the rocks.

"It's going to be tricky," he said. "We'll have to go slowly and carefully." Slowly, rock by rock they moved forward, until suddenly "Get back!" cried a voice. "Cave in!"

The second fall filled the hole again, but luckily no one was hurt. Tony and Mitch heard Diana scream, "What can you do now, Mr Taylor?"

"Nothing here," said Big Jim. "It's too dangerous." Tony and Mitch heard the men's footsteps grow fainter as they left the cave.

"Oh God!" said Tony in despair, "we're going to die. They've given up and left us."

Outside the cave Big Jim turned to the other men. "We must look around. We know they are in the old mine. There must be another way in."

"Don't worry!" Diana called back into the cave. "We'll get you out." But her voice was lost in the wind and the waves, and Tony and Mitch heard nothing.

After the rescue party had gone a few metres they met the farmer.
"Yes, there is another entrance," he said. "Come with me."

"I know every centimetre of this country. They must be in the old copper mine. There is a shaft for the old lifting gear, but it's very dangerous and no one goes near it these days."

"Take us there as quickly as you can," said Big Jim. "They may be running out of air."
Diana began to cry quietly to herself.

They scrambled up over the rocks, and through clumps of gorse and heather, until at last they saw the dark mass of broken machinery standing out in the dim light.

At the edge of the gaping hole in the ground they got ready to lower one man down into the mine. As they stood by, waiting, the earth began to crumble and slowly slide into the hole.

"It's no good," said Big Jim. "We'll need special gear." "But that will take time," pleaded Diana. "We may be too late, and . . ."

Big Jim took no notice. Already he was on his way back to the Special Rescue Headquarters.

Down in the tunnel where Mitch and Tony were trapped, the air grew thicker, but the water level had not risen higher.
"I feel worse now," said Tony.

"The air is getting bad," said Mitch. "We can't stay here much longer. Let's explore the cave once more."

They groped about until they came to the pile of stones. "We'll try again. Perhaps we can move some smaller rocks and make a hole large enough to let in some fresh air."

Mitch used his hammer and removed a number of rocks. Tony, still in pain, tried to help using his right arm. Soon Tony was exhausted.

"Mitch, it's getting darker, my battery has gone . . ."
His voice trailed away into a horrified gasp, then rose to a shriek.
"There's something moving about, I can feel it!"

"Oh, it's only a small animal—probably a rat or something." Tony shivered. Mitch was still hammering at the rocks but none would move.
"We're stuck!" he said.

On the hill Big Jim had returned with the special rescue truck and heavy equipment. Soon Diana and the rescue team were lowered into the mine.

At the bottom of the shaft they saw abandoned trolleys, broken timber and falls of rock, before they made out three tunnels leading away into the old workings.

"We'll try the right-hand one first," said Big Jim. After a few metres, the tunnel was completely blocked, and they had to return to the main shaft.

Diana was really afraid now. She wondered if they would ever find Tony and Mitch. They chose the smaller centre tunnel next.

The wooden props holding up the roof groaned at the slightest touch. Small stones fell, and water dripped and splashed into puddles on the floor.

Suddenly, a pit prop gave way and a section of the roof fell in with a terrific roar.

One of the men was trapped. The others removed a large rock and found that his leg was badly crushed.

"Leave me," he said. "You must find the others. They need help more than I do."

Big Jim made him comfortable in a safe place, and then scrambling over falls of rock, they hurried on until they were stopped by a pile of rocks.

"Make a hole quickly! This may be the place," said Big Jim.

Tony was very sick and in great pain by now. Mitch took off his coat, and gave him the rest of the coffee to make him more comfortable.

"You go to sleep," he said. "I'll let you know if I hear anything." Almost as he spoke, he heard the low rumble of a rock-fall.

It grew louder and louder. When it ended he began to tap the rock wall with his hammer. Three loud taps—three soft ones, again and again.

Out in the tunnel Big Jim put up his hand.
"Stop work, I can hear something!"
They listened, and heard the faint sounds of Mitch hammering on the rock.

"We've found them!" cried Diana, tears of joy streaming down her face. Then she answered Mitch's call with three loud and three soft taps until she was sure he had heard.

Soon they had broken through the wall of rock and Big Jim crawled through. "Bring a stretcher," he said. "The lad is hurt."

Diana bent down and looked at Tony's pale face as he lay on the stretcher. Then she gently touched his face just to make sure that he was still alive. It felt warm against her hand.

Two of the men carried Tony out on the stretcher. "Hurry," said Big Jim. "There is another fall coming."

"Look out!" screamed Diana as a great rush of water poured through the roof. All around them, they could hear the sound of falling rock and rushing water.

They hurried to the bottom of the shaft, where already the water level was creeping up. By the dim light of their lamps they were all hauled up to safety.

First Tony on the stretcher. Then Diana and Mitch with the rescuers. Big Jim came up last, just as the water was about to rise over his shoulders.

Over by the light Mitch examined a piece of rock. "It's copper, all right," he said. "A rich vein, but I think it would be too dangerous to mine it." They all nodded in agreement.

Tony, wrapped up in the warm blankets on the stretcher, was beginning to feel better. Diana gave him another cup of hot coffee.

"You know," he said, "I think I like a day underground. I think I'll go pot-holing again one day when my arm is better."

"Well, I'm blowed!" said Big Jim, as they drove away from the farm.
"Some people never learn." Then he laughed.

Things To Do

1 Put the following words into your work book:
explore dangerous specimens unconscious information entrance abandoned examined comfortable desperately

2 Put each word into a sentence so that it tells something about the story.

3 Look at page 27, then copy the sentences below into your work book and put in the missing words. Tony was very . . . and in great . . . by now. . . . took off his . . . and gave him the rest of the . . . to make him more . . .
"You go to . . ." he said. "I'll let you know if . . . ." Almost as he . . ., he heard the . . . . . . of a . . .-. . .

4 Write words in your work book to fit the following meanings. Each word will be found on the page shown at the end of each sentence.
a A man who studies rocks. (page 2)
b Tied firmly to something. (page 6)
c Without any way of escape. (page 9)
d Below the surface of the earth. (page 10)
e To give up hope. (page 18)
f Way into a place. (page 19)
g Hole leading into a mine. (page 24)

5 You are Tony. Write to Big Jim and thank him for saving your life.

6 You are Diana. Write to the farmer's wife and thank her for helping you.

This edition © 1976 Macmillan Education Ltd
Original edition © 1973 Alwyn Cox
Reprinted 1979

Published by Macmillan Education Ltd, Basingstoke and London
Printed in Hong Kong